2017 SQA Specimen and Past Papers with Answers

National 5
COMPUTING SCIENCE

2016 & 2017 Exams
and 2017 Specimen Question Paper

HODDER
GIBSON
AN HACHETTE UK COMPANY

This book contains the official SQA 2016 and 2017 Exams and the 2017 Specimen Question Paper for National 5 Computing Science, with associated SQA-approved answers modified from the official marking instructions that accompany the paper.

In addition the book contains study skills advice. This advice has been specially commissioned by Hodder Gibson, and has been written by experienced senior teachers and examiners in line with the new National 5 syllabus and assessment outlines. This is not SQA material but has been devised to provide further guidance for National 5 examinations.

Hodder Gibson is grateful to the copyright holders for permission to use their material. Every effort has been made to trace the copyright holders and to obtain their permission for the use of copyright material. Hodder Gibson will be happy to receive information allowing us to rectify any error or omission in future editions.

Permission has been sought from all relevant copyright holders and Hodder Gibson is grateful for the use of the following:

Image © JMiks/Shutterstock.com (2016 page 4);
Image © nikifiva/Shutterstock.com (2016 page 5);
Image © Tatiana Popova/Shutterstock.com (2016 page 5);
Image © Linusy/Shutterstock.com (2016 page 7);
Image © Neirfy/Shutterstock.com (2016 pages 18 & 19);
Image © Zern Liew/Shutterstock.com (2016 pages 20 & 21);
Image © Erik Lam/stock.adobe.com (2017 page 3);
Two images © Menno Schaefer/Shutterstock.com (2017 page 27);
Image © Neirfy/Shutterstock.com (2017 SQP page 8);
Image © Lucky Images/Shutterstock.com (2017 SQP page 8);
Image © Wavebreakmedia/stock.adobe.com (2017 SQP page 8);
Image © gstockstudio/stock.adobe.com (2017 SQP page 14);
Image © Egoreichenkov Evgenii/Shutterstock.com (2017 SQP pages 16 & 18).

Hachette UK's policy is to use papers that are natural, renewable and recyclable products and made from wood grown in sustainable forests. The logging and manufacturing processes are expected to conform to the environmental regulations of the country of origin.

Orders: please contact Bookpoint Ltd, 130 Park Drive, Milton Park, Abingdon, Oxon OX14 4SE. Telephone: (44) 01235 827720. Fax: (44) 01235 400454. Lines are open 9.00–5.00, Monday to Saturday, with a 24-hour message answering service. Visit our website at www.hoddereducation.co.uk. Hodder Gibson can be contacted direct on: Tel: 0141 333 4650; Fax: 0141 404 8188; email: hoddergibson@hodder.co.uk

This collection first published in 2017 by
Hodder Gibson, an imprint of Hodder Education,
An Hachette UK Company
211 St Vincent Street
Glasgow G2 5QY

Typeset by Aptara, Inc.

Printed in the UK

A catalogue record for this title is available from the British Library

ISBN: 978-1-5104-2160-8

2 1

2018 2017

Introduction

National 5 Computing Science

This book of SQA past papers contains the question papers used in the 2016 and 2017 exams (with answers at the back of the book). The National 5 Computing Science exam is being extended by 20 marks for 2018 onwards, following the removal of unit assessments from the course. A new specimen question paper, which reflects the requirements of the revised exam, is also included. The specimen question paper reflects the content and duration of the exam in 2018.

All of the question papers included in the book (2016, 2017 and the new specimen question paper) provide excellent representative exam practice for the final exams. Using the 2016 and 2017 past papers as part of your revision will help you to develop the vital skills and techniques needed for the exam, and will help you to identify any knowledge gaps you may have.

It is always a very good idea to refer to SQA's website for the most up-to-date course specification documents. These are available for each subject at www.sqa.org.uk/nqsubjects

The exam

The marks for the examination are distributed across all the four areas that you will have studied.

Approximately 40% of the marks in the question paper will be awarded to Software design and development; approximately 10% of the marks will be awarded to Computer systems. Approximately 25% of the marks will be awarded to Database design and development, and the remaining 25% will be awarded to Web design and development.

Section 1 will have 25 marks and will consist of short answered questions assessing the breadth of knowledge across all four areas.

Section 2 will have 85 marks and consist of structured questions. These questions will be context-based from all four areas. Very few of these questions will require direct recall of knowledge, the solutions to questions will require some descriptions and explanations, some questions will be integrated across two or more topics.

Questions relating to *Software design and development* will cover the following areas:

- Development methodologies
- Analysis
- Design
- Implementation (data types and structures, computational constructs, algorithm specification)
- Testing
- Evaluation

Questions relating to *Computer systems* will cover the following areas:

- Data representation
- Computer structure
- Environmental impact
- Security precautions

Questions relating to *Database design and development* will cover the following areas:

- Analysis
- Design
- Implementation
- Testing
- Evaluation

Questions relating to *Web design and development* will cover the following areas:

- Analysis
- Design
- Implementation (CSS, HTML, Javascript)
- Testing
- Evaluation

General advice

Remember to prepare for the exam by making sure you have revised all areas in the SQA 'Skills, knowledge and understanding for the course assignment' section of the National 5 Course Specification for Computing Science.

In the exam read the question very carefully and answer only what is being asked. It is important that you refer to the context of the question when answering.

Where you are required to answer questions by writing in code, you can answer the questions using any programming language; marks are awarded for demonstrating your understanding and the efficiency of your solution, not for the correct use of syntax. SQA's standardised reference language is used to ask questions to assess your understanding and application of programming skills (but you are not expected to answer questions using SQA standardised reference language).

Software design and development

You are required to be able to describe, identify, read and understand all of the following three designs – structured diagrams, flow charts and pseudocode – BUT you only need to use one design technique to implement an efficient solution to a problem.

In National 5 Computing Science, you have three standard algorithms that you must be able to describe and exemplify in the examination. You need to be able to apply these algorithms in a range of contexts: input validation, running total within loop, and traversing a 1-D array.

Database design and development

You are required for the exam to be able to apply knowledge of entity relationship diagrams data dictionaries and exemplify designs of solutions to queries for a variety of contexts. In these questions read all the parts and information provided very carefully. You will also be required to read and explain SQL code; this may also require you to edit or finish SQL code to demonstrate your understanding.

Web design and development

You are required for the exam to be able to consider the end user and develop wire frames for a variety of contexts; if developing a wire frame, ensure you read the question and make sure you include all relevant information including media types.

In the exam you could be required to demonstrate your knowledge of CSS and HTML within a context.

Computers and the Law

The National 5 Computing science exam requires you to have knowledge of the Copyright, Designs and Patents Act1 988 and the Data Protection Act 1998.

Trade names

It is never acceptable to use a company name, such as Microsoft Access or Serif Web-Plus etc. in an answer. Use the generic terms such as databases or web-design packages.

Conversion

If you are asked to convert a number into an 8-bit binary number, make sure that your answer has 8 bits!

Technical terminology

It is important that the correct technical terminology is used, e.g. USB flash drive – not USB pen, USB stick, pen drive or other commonly used expressions.

Units

Remember, there are 1024 bytes in a Kilobyte, not 1000. There are:

- 1024 Kilobytes in a Megabyte
- 1024 Megabytes in a Gigabyte
- 1024 Gigabytes in a Terabyte.

Memory

Many candidates confuse RAM memory with backing storage. Remember, RAM memory is used to store programs and data temporarily while the program is being used. Backing storage is used to hold programs and data permanently until you are ready to use them. When you open an application it is taken from the backing storage (e.g. hard disc drive) and placed into the RAM memory.

Calculating storage requirements

When calculating the storage requirements for photographs, too many candidates forget that DPI must be squared. Remember to multiply the number of bits required to store the colour – NOT the number of colours!

For example, an image measures 3 inches by 4 inches and has a resolution of 600dpi in 8 colours

= 3 x 4 x 600 x 600 x 3 (3 bits can give 8 combinations of colours)

= 12960000 bits = 12960000/8 =1620000 bytes

= 1620000/1024 = 1582.03 Kb = 1882.03 / 1024

= 1.54 Mb

Computers and the law

Candidates must give the correct full names of the appropriate laws and be able to give description, identification and implications for individuals and businesses for the "Data Protection Act", "Computer Misuse Act", "Health & Safety Regulations", "Communications Act" and "Copyright, Design and Patents Act".

Interfaces

Many candidates forget why an interface is required. Remember that an interface changes electrical voltages, changes analogue to digital, buffers data and deals with control signals. DO NOT confuse it with the Human Computer Interface.

Pre-defined functions

Remember that pre-defined functions (with parameters) are built-in sections of code that have been written and tested and are available for programmers to use. They include random, integer and round.

Good luck!

Remember that the rewards for passing National 5 Computing Science are well worth it! Your pass will help you get the future you want for yourself. In the exam, be confident in your own ability. If you're not sure how to answer a question, trust your instincts and just give it a go anyway. Keep calm and don't panic! GOOD LUCK!

Study Skills – what you need to know to pass exams!

Pause for thought

Many students might skip quickly through a page like this. After all, we all know how to revise. Do you really though?

Think about this:

"IF YOU ALWAYS DO WHAT YOU ALWAYS DO, YOU WILL ALWAYS GET WHAT YOU HAVE ALWAYS GOT."

Do you like the grades you get? Do you want to do better? If you get full marks in your assessment, then that's great! Change nothing! This section is just to help you get that little bit better than you already are.

There are two main parts to the advice on offer here. The first part highlights fairly obvious things but which are also very important. The second part makes suggestions about revision that you might not have thought about but which WILL help you.

Part 1

DOH! It's so obvious but …

Start revising in good time

Don't leave it until the last minute – this will make you panic.

Make a revision timetable that sets out work time AND play time.

Sleep and eat!

Obvious really, and very helpful. Avoid arguments or stressful things too – even games that wind you up. You need to be fit, awake and focused!

Know your place!

Make sure you know exactly **WHEN and WHERE** your exams are.

Know your enemy!

Make sure you know what to expect in the exam.

How is the paper structured?

How much time is there for each question?

What types of question are involved?

Which topics seem to come up time and time again?

Which topics are your strongest and which are your weakest?

Are all topics compulsory or are there choices?

Learn by DOING!

There is no substitute for past papers and practice papers – they are simply essential! Tackling this collection of papers and answers is exactly the right thing to be doing as your exams approach.

Part 2

People learn in different ways. Some like low light, some bright. Some like early morning, some like evening / night. Some prefer warm, some prefer cold. But everyone uses their BRAIN and the brain works when it is active. Passive learning – sitting gazing at notes – is the most INEFFICIENT way to learn anything. Below you will find tips and ideas for making your revision more effective and maybe even more enjoyable. What follows gets your brain active, and active learning works!

Activity 1 – Stop and review

Step 1

When you have done no more than 5 minutes of revision reading STOP!

Step 2

Write a heading in your own words which sums up the topic you have been revising.

Step 3

Write a summary of what you have revised in no more than two sentences. Don't fool yourself by saying, "I know it, but I cannot put it into words". That just means you don't know it well enough. If you cannot write your summary, revise that section again, knowing that you must write a summary at the end of it. Many of you will have notebooks full of blue/black ink writing. Many of the pages will not be especially attractive or memorable so try to liven them up a bit with colour as you are reviewing and rewriting. **This is a great memory aid, and memory is the most important thing.**

Activity 2 – Use technology!

Why should everything be written down? Have you thought about "mental" maps, diagrams, cartoons and colour to help you learn? And rather than write down notes, why not record your revision material?

What about having a text message revision session with friends? Keep in touch with them to find out how and what they are revising and share ideas and questions.

Why not make a video diary where you tell the camera what you are doing, what you think you have learned and what you still have to do? No one has to see or hear it, but the process of having to organise your thoughts in a formal way to explain something is a very important learning practice.

Be sure to make use of electronic files. You could begin to summarise your class notes. Your typing might be slow, but it will get faster and the typed notes will be easier to read than the scribbles in your class notes. Try to add different fonts and colours to make your work stand out. You can easily Google relevant pictures, cartoons and diagrams which you can copy and paste to make your work more attractive and **MEMORABLE**.

Activity 3 – This is it. Do this and you will know lots!

Step 1

In this task you must be very honest with yourself! Find the SQA syllabus for your subject (www.sqa.org.uk). Look at how it is broken down into main topics called MANDATORY knowledge. That means stuff you MUST know.

Step 2

BEFORE you do ANY revision on this topic, write a list of everything that you already know about the subject. It might be quite a long list but you only need to write it once. It shows you all the information that is already in your long-term memory so you know what parts you do not need to revise!

Step 3

Pick a chapter or section from your book or revision notes. Choose a fairly large section or a whole chapter to get the most out of this activity.

With a buddy, use Skype, Facetime, Twitter or any other communication you have, to play the game "If this is the answer, what is the question?". For example, if you are revising Geography and the answer you provide is "meander", your buddy would have to make up a question like "What is the word that describes a feature of a river where it flows slowly and bends often from side to side?".

Make up 10 "answers" based on the content of the chapter or section you are using. Give this to your buddy to solve while you solve theirs.

Step 4

Construct a wordsearch of at least 10 × 10 squares. You can make it as big as you like but keep it realistic. Work together with a group of friends. Many apps allow you to make wordsearch puzzles online. The words and phrases can go in any direction and phrases can be split. Your puzzle must only contain facts linked to the topic you are revising. Your task is to find 10 bits of information to hide in your puzzle, but you must not repeat information that you used in Step 3. DO NOT show where the words are. Fill up empty squares with random letters. Remember to keep a note of where your answers are hidden but do not show your friends. When you have a complete puzzle, exchange it with a friend to solve each other's puzzle.

Step 5

Now make up 10 questions (not "answers" this time) based on the same chapter used in the previous two tasks. Again, you must find NEW information that you have not yet used. Now it's getting hard to find that new information! Again, give your questions to a friend to answer.

Step 6

As you have been doing the puzzles, your brain has been actively searching for new information. Now write a NEW LIST that contains only the new information you have discovered when doing the puzzles. Your new list is the one to look at repeatedly for short bursts over the next few days. Try to remember more and more of it without looking at it. After a few days, you should be able to add words from your second list to your first list as you increase the information in your long-term memory.

FINALLY! Be inspired...

Make a list of different revision ideas and beside each one write **THINGS I HAVE** tried, **THINGS I WILL** try and **THINGS I MIGHT** try. Don't be scared of trying something new.

And remember – "FAIL TO PREPARE AND PREPARE TO FAIL!"

NATIONAL 5

2016

National
Qualifications
2016

Mark

X716/75/01

Computing Science

FRIDAY, 27 MAY

1:00 PM — 2:30 PM

Fill in these boxes and read what is printed below.

Full name of centre

Town

Forename(s)

Surname

Number of seat

Date of birth

Day   Month   Year   Scottish candidate number

Total marks — 90

SECTION 1 — 20 marks

Attempt ALL questions.

SECTION 2 — 70 marks

Attempt ALL questions.

Show all working.

Write your answers clearly in the spaces provided in this booklet. Additional space for answers is provided at the end of this booklet. If you use this space you must clearly identify the question number you are attempting.

Use **blue** or **black** ink.

Before leaving the examination room you must give this booklet to the Invigilator; if you do not, you may lose all the marks for this paper.

MARKS | DO NOT WRITE IN THIS MARGIN

SECTION 1 — 20 MARKS

Attempt ALL Questions

1. Convert the decimal value 227 into the equivalent 8-bit binary number.   **1**

2. Explain why it is important that program code is readable.   **1**

_____

_____

3. Explain why a **database** should not be stored in ROM memory.   **1**

_____

_____

_____

_____

MARKS | DO NOT WRITE IN THIS MARGIN

4. Give **one** reason for using this type of selection.

    ◯ OPTION 1 - Yes

    👉◉ OPTION 2 - No

    ◯ OPTION 3 - Not Sure   1

    _____

    _____

    _____

    _____

5. State the function of a processor's registers.   1

    _____

    _____

                                    [Turn over

6. Anti-virus software may be included in a security suite.

State **two** other types of software which should be included in a security suite.

2

1 _____

_____

2 _____

_____

7. Criminals can steal your identity by using keylogger programs. State **two** other ways in which identity theft can be carried out.

2

1 _____

_____

2 _____

_____

MARKS | DO NOT WRITE IN THIS MARGIN

8. A novice is one type of user of an information system.

State **one** other type of user.   1

_____

9. This code design monitors the temperature of food as it is reheated.

Line 1   RECEIVE temperature FROM (REAL) *<temperature sensor>*

Line 2   WHILE temperature < 82 DO

Line 3   SEND "temperature too low: continue to reheat" TO DISPLAY

Line 4   RECEIVE temperature FROM (REAL) *<temperature sensor>*

Line 5   END WHILE

Explain what will happen in lines 2 to 5 if the sensor detects 63°.   2

_____

_____

_____

_____

_____

_____

_____

10. Lucy is looking for a summer holiday on-line. She wishes to leave on 22nd July from her local airport, and early in the afternoon.

State which database operation is being carried out as she uses the website.   1

_____

MARKS | DO NOT WRITE IN THIS MARGIN

11. Translators are used to convert high level languages into machine code.

Identify each type of translator.

	Type of Translator
This translator program reports errors at the end of translation.	
This translator needs to be present in memory each time the program is executed.	

2

12. A running group has 16 members. They are taking part in a marathon.

Using pseudocode or a programming language of your choice, write the code which will take in each runner's time for the marathon.

2

13. Before launching the website below, it is tested. The testers complain about the effectiveness of the website's navigation.

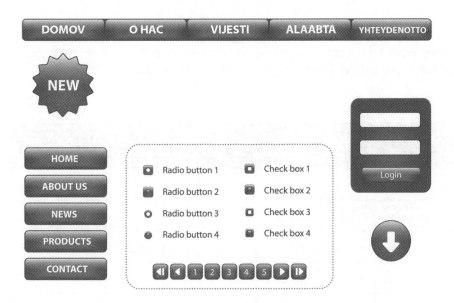

Identify **two** examples of poor navigation, stating what could be done to improve the situation.

2

1 _____

_____

_____

_____

2 _____

_____

_____

_____

14. State the **type** of network which has no centralised storage.

1

_____

[Turn over

SECTION 2 — 70 MARKS

Attempt ALL Questions

15. FlightCrazy is a new company offering a flight booking service to business customers. They want to set up a database to store flight details. A researcher starts to gather information from airport timetables about available flight times.

Route ID	Departure Airport	Destination Airport	Day	Departure Time	Duration (hrs)	Airline Ref	Airline Name	Flight Number	Aircraft Code
001	Edinburgh	Amsterdam	Monday	07:00	01:35	KL	KLM	KL1276	737
001	Edinburgh	Amsterdam	Monday	08:00	01:30	U2	Easyjet	U26921	319
001	Edinburgh	Amsterdam	Saturday	10:15	01:30	U2	Easyjet	U26921	320
001	Edin	Amsterdam	Monday	11:10	01:30	KL	KLM	KL1280	737
001	Edinburgh	Ams	Tuesday	07:00	01:35	KL	KLM	KL1276	737
003	Edinburgh	London Heathrow	Monday	08:00	01:35	BA	British Airways	BA1461	EQV
002	Edinburgh	London Gatwick	Mon	06:40	01:35	BA	British Airways	BA2931	EQV
002	Edin	London GAT	Sat	06:25	01:30	U2	Easyjet	U2802	EQV
003	Edinburgh	Heathrow	Monday	09:10	01:30	VS	Virgin Atlantic	VS3002	320

(a) If the full database is created as a flat file, explain why "RouteID" is not a suitable primary key for the table.

1

_____

_____

MARKS | DO NOT WRITE IN THIS MARGIN

15. **(continued)**

(b) Describe **two** problems in creating this as a flat file database.   2

Problem 1

_____

_____

_____

Problem 2

_____

_____

_____

(c) FlightCrazy decided that using a flat file database is not suitable.
State a more suitable type of database.   1

_____

(d) State the **field type** that should be used for "Aircraft Code".   1

_____

[Turn over

15. **(continued)**

(e) During the development of this database the following input form is created.

Search for a flight

Departure Airport *   Edinburgh ▼

Destination Airport *

- ◉ One way   ○ Return

| Edinburgh |
| Glasgow |
| Aberdeen |
| Dundee |
| Inverness |
| Wick |

Departure time

Date of travel *

Number of travellers *   (max 6)

Find Flights

* indicates field cannot be left empty

(i) State **one** suitable type of validation for the Departure Airport field.

    1

_____

(ii) Complete the table below to show suitable data values to test the Number of travellers field.

    2

Type of Test data	Test data
Exceptional	
Extreme	

MARKS | DO NOT WRITE IN THIS MARGIN

15.   (continued)

(f)   During the testing of the completed database all the flights from Glasgow to all airports in London on the 8th June were found. The following output was produced.

11 flights match your search criteria				
From:	Glasgow	To:	London	
Date:	8th June			
Depart	Destination	Journey Time	Price	Airline
21:20	LTN	1h10	39	Easyjet
21:45	LGW	1h25	39	Easyjet
20:45	STN	1h20	40	Ryanair
06:30	STN	1h15	47	Easyjet
19:55	STN	1h15	47	Easyjet
21:00	LHR	1h15	47	British Airways
07:00	LTN	1h10	57	Easyjet
07:05	STN	1h20	57	Ryanair
09:20	LTN	1h10	57	Easyjet
10:25	STN	1h15	57	Ryanair
09:25	LGW	1h25	73	British Airways

Describe how the above results have been sorted.   2

_____

_____

_____

[Turn over

16. A Maths game is designed for primary school pupils to test number ordering. In the game the pupil is asked to enter two integer numbers. A third integer number is then randomly generated and shown to the user.

The user must then state if the random number is:

lower (l) than the two entered numbers
higher (h) than the two entered numbers
in the middle (m) of the two entered numbers.

A design for the code is shown below.

Line 1   *<enter the first number and assign to numOne>*
Line 2   *<enter the second number and assign to numTwo>*
Line 3   *<generate random number and assign to randNum>*
Line 4   SEND randNum TO DISPLAY
Line 5   RECEIVE guess FROM (CHARACTER) KEYBOARD
Line 6   IF guess = "l" AND randNum < numOne THEN
Line 7   SEND "Correct it is lower" TO DISPLAY
Line 8   SET score TO score + 1
Line 9   END IF
Line 10   IF guess = "m" AND randNum >= numOne AND randNum <= numTwo
Line 11   SEND "Correct it is in the middle" TO DISPLAY
Line 12   SET score TO score + 1
Line 13   END IF
Line 14   IF guess = "h" AND randNum > numTwo
Line 15   SEND "Correct it is higher" TO DISPLAY
Line 16   SET score TO score + 1
Line 17   END IF
Line 18   *<display incorrect message>*

(a) When the two numbers are entered the program should ensure that numTwo is always a higher number than numOne.

Using pseudocode or a programming language of your choice, write several lines to represent this input validation for line 2.   4

MARKS | DO NOT WRITE IN THIS MARGIN

16. (continued)

(b) When the pupil enters the answer it is stored in a variable called "guess".

State the **data type** stored by the variable "guess".   1

_____

(c) The program is run with the following data.

Variables	Values
numOne	7
numTwo	15
randNum	10
guess	m

State the output from the program.   1

_____

_____

_____

_____

(d) The program will have to make use of a pre-defined function.

State the pre-defined function used and describe its purpose.   2

_____

_____

(e) Using line numbers, describe how the code could be adapted, allowing the user to play the game 10 times using the same values for numOne and numTwo but a different random number each time.   2

_____

_____

_____

_____

_____

MARKS | DO NOT WRITE IN THIS MARGIN

17. John has been asked to design a website to promote an event being held to raise money for charity.

The organisers of the event provide this diagram showing the pages required and how they should be organised.

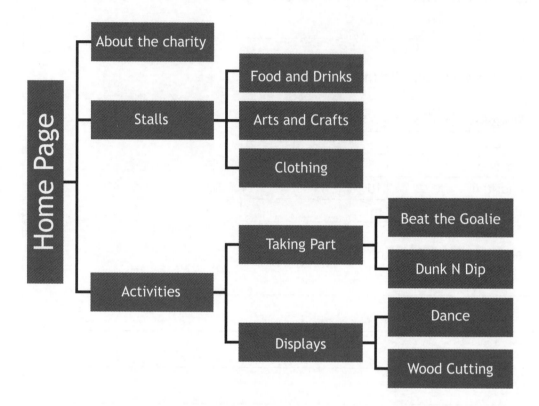

(a) What **type** of navigation structure is required for the website?   1

_____

_____

(b) State a design notation that John could use to design the layout of the pages.   1

_____

_____

(c) The homepage contains hyperlinks. Describe the function of a hyperlink.   1

_____

_____

_____

17. (continued)

(d) John begins to build the website and stores all the files and resources on his hard disk.

Here is the file structure for the website.

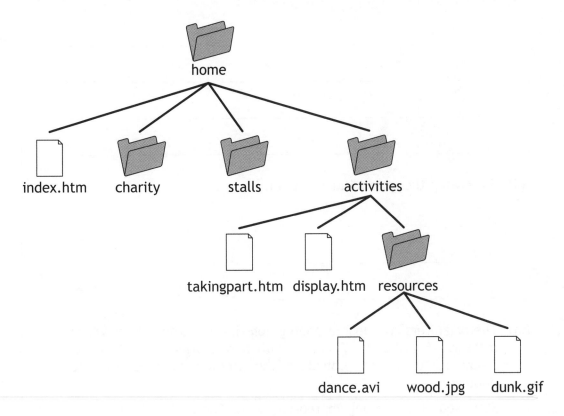

MARKS

(i) State the type of data you would expect to be stored in the dance.avi file.

1

_____

(ii) State the **relative** address John should enter on the display.htm page to link to dunk.gif.

1

_____

_____

[Turn over

MARKS | DO NOT WRITE IN THIS MARGIN

17. (continued)

(e) John wants to include an external link to the charity and asks the event organisers to find out the URL.

(i) Explain what is meant by an external link.

1

(ii) State what the letters URL stand for.

1

U _____

R _____

L _____

(iii) The organisers give John a photograph file from the charity which measures 5 inches by 7 inches with a resolution of 600dpi and 24-bit colour depth. Calculate the storage required for the photograph.

State your answer using appropriate units. Show all your working.

3

MARKS | DO NOT WRITE IN THIS MARGIN

18. A software development company decides to review staff knowledge of computer related legislation.

Mikal is asked to create an app covering a range of legal issues.

(a) When Mikal records an introduction using audio software, he is prompted to select the sample rate.

Select sampling rate:

○ 22050 Hz
○ 44100 Hz
○ 96000 Hz

(i) Describe the effect on the size of the sound file if the highest sample rate is selected.

1

_____

_____

_____

(ii) After recording, Mikal exports the file as a compressed file.

State a suitable standard file format he may have used.

1

_____

[Turn over

MARKS | DO NOT WRITE IN THIS MARGIN

18. (continued)

(b) Mikal develops an interactive quiz for the app to test the staff's knowledge of legislation. The first question is about this recent article from a newspaper.

MONDAY
may, 20 2013

NEWS

№ 34747/53

Only fresh news   founded 1953

An office worker has been disciplined for accessing the company's email system using the login and password of another employee, without permission, and reading the private emails of the Chief Executive Officer.

(i) State the offence that has been committed under the Computer Misuse Act in this article.   **1**

_____

_____

(ii) Describe another offence under the terms of this Act.   **1**

_____

_____

MARKS | DO NOT WRITE IN THIS MARGIN

18. **(continued)**

(c) The next question that Mikal creates for the quiz is about another article.

MONDAY
may, 20 2013

NEWS

№ 34747/53

Only fresh news   founded 1953

A man was arrested after he cloned his neighbour's phone.

Name the law which may have been broken in this case.   1

_____

_____

[Turn over

MARKS | DO NOT WRITE IN THIS MARGIN

18.   (continued)

(d) In line with Health and Safety legislation, the company provides adjustable seating and guidelines on maintaining good posture.

Mikal finds graphics on a website that he can use to illustrate his next quiz question.

(i) Explain why he might need to seek permission to use the graphics legally.

1

_____

_____

18. (d) (continued)

(ii) Mikal uses the graphics to create question 3 for the app.

Using pseudocode or a programming language of your choice, write the code to show how the total score is calculated when the user answers question 3 correctly.

2

MARKS | DO NOT WRITE IN THIS MARGIN

18.   **(continued)**

(e) When the staff member runs the finished quiz, the app sends their details and their total score to a database file.

State **two** rights that the staff member has under the Data Protection Act with regard to their own data.

2

_____

_____

_____

_____

_____

MARKS | DO NOT WRITE IN THIS MARGIN

19. Gillian designs a program to calculate how much it costs to get her dog Penny groomed. The design is shown below.

Line 1   SET total = 0
Line 2   DECLARE all costs INITIALLY [35.00, 36.00, 40.00, 35.00, 42.50]
Line 3   FOR EACH cost FROM all costs DUE
Line 4   SET total=total+cost
Line 5   END FOR EACH
Line 6   SEND "The total cost = £"&total TO DISPLAY

(a) Describe the data structure that has been used to store the individual costs.

2

_____

_____

(b) Gillian writes and tests her program. It works perfectly calculating a correct total of 188.50.

(i) With reference to line numbers, explain how the program calculates the final total.

3

_____

_____

_____

_____

_____

_____

(ii) Describe how the contents of the variable total would be stored in the computer's memory.

2

_____

_____

[Turn over

MARKS | DO NOT WRITE IN THIS MARGIN

19. (b) (continued)

(iii) Gillian edits the program with the following data:
[35.00, 36.00, 40.00, 35.00, 42.50, **45.00**]
The output is still 188.50.

A   Explain why the output is still 188.50.   1

_____

B   State how this error could be corrected.   1

_____

(c) Concatenation has been used in line 6.

State the purpose of concatenation.   1

_____

_____

_____

[Turn over for next question

DO NOT WRITE ON THIS PAGE

MARKS | DO NOT WRITE IN THIS MARGIN

20. Sue uses a website called "Check your Defences!" to learn more about keeping her computer and data safe.

(a) Explain the purpose of a firewall. **1**

_____

_____

(b) Explain how encryption can help keep data safe. **2**

_____

_____

_____

_____

_____

_____

MARKS | DO NOT WRITE IN THIS MARGIN

20.   (continued)

When Sue tries to download the mobile app onto her tablet PC, she gets the following message:

 This app is incompatible with your device

Check your Defences!
System requirements
Android 4·4 or higher
1·6 GHz
2Gb RAM
32 GB

She checks the specification for her tablet PC.

> Size: 267 x 187 x 8 mm
> Weight: 0·65 kg
> 1·83 GHz/2 GB RAM/16 GB
> Battery life: up to 8 hours
> Display: 8·3" full HD, 10 point multi-touch
> Operating system: Android 4·1
> USB 3·0, micro HDMI, microSD card slot
> 3·5 MP camera
> Microphone
> Stereo speakers
> Headphone jack
> Wi-Fi

(c)   (i)   Sue's tablet has a range of input and output devices. Identify **one** of each of these items on Sue's tablet.   2

Input device_____

_____

Output device_____

_____

(ii)   Identify **one** interface type on Sue's tablet.   1

Interface type_____

_____

MARKS | DO NOT WRITE IN THIS MARGIN

20. **(c)** **(continued)**

(iii) Describe **one** function of an interface.   1

_____

_____

_____

(iv) Give **two** reasons why the app is incompatible with Sue's tablet PC.   2

Reason 1 _____

_____

_____

Reason 2 _____

_____

_____

MARKS

20.   (continued)

(d) Sue's friend Jack views the website on his smart phone but the home screen looks different to the desktop version Sue had been using.

Smartphone version   Desktop version

Describe **one** reason why the user interface on the smartphone version is designed differently to the version Sue had used on her desktop.   1

_____

_____

_____

[Turn over

MARKS | DO NOT WRITE IN THIS MARGIN

21. A software developer is creating an online booking system for a bowling alley. Customers can book a bowling lane for a maximum of 4 people playing a maximum of 3 games.

The developer has used a flow chart to produce the program design. Part of the design is shown below.

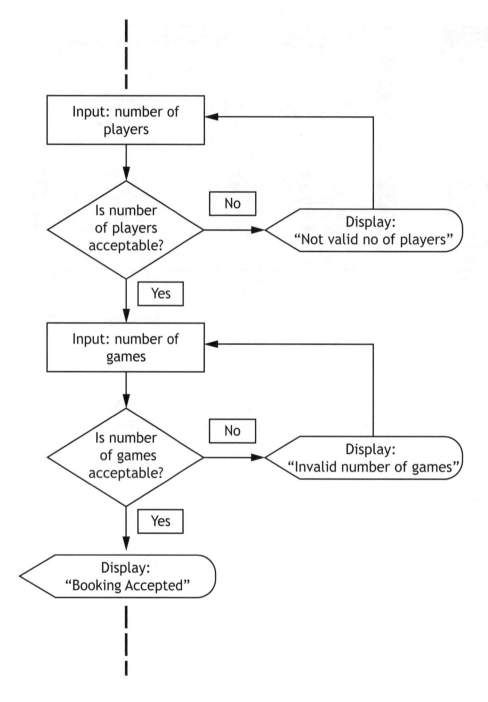

(a) (i) State **one** benefit of using the design notation shown above instead of pseudocode.

1

_____

_____

MARKS | DO NOT WRITE IN THIS MARGIN

21. (a) (continued)

(ii) Name the algorithm illustrated in the bowling alley program design. **1**

_____

_____

(b)

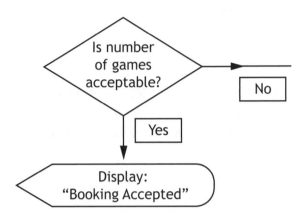

Using pseudocode or a programming language of your choice, complete the conditional statement at Line 3 below to implement this section of the design. **3**

Line 3 _____ numPlayers _____ and

numGames _____

Line 4 SEND "Booking Accepted" TO DISPLAY

(c) The program is tested using a set of test data.

(i) Complete the table below to show three examples of test data types and the expected result for each type. **3**

Test data	Test data type	Expected Result
numPlayers = 3 numGames = 2	Normal	Booking accepted
numPlayers = 4 numGames = 3		Booking accepted
numPlayers = 6 numGames = 3		

MARKS | DO NOT WRITE IN THIS MARGIN

21. (c) (continued)

(ii) The character "£" is entered as a test value for the number of players. This causes the program to crash.

State the **type** of error that would cause this crash.

1

_____

_____

(d) Error detection and correction in a program is easier if the code is readable.

State **one** technique that can be used to ensure *readability* of code.

1

_____

_____

[END OF QUESTION PAPER]

MARKS | DO NOT WRITE IN THIS MARGIN

ADDITIONAL SPACE FOR ANSWERS

MARKS | DO NOT WRITE IN THIS MARGIN

ADDITIONAL SPACE FOR ANSWERS

NATIONAL 5

2017

N5

National Qualifications 2017

Mark

X716/75/01

Computing Science

TUESDAY, 16 MAY

1:00 PM — 2:30 PM

Fill in these boxes and read what is printed below.

Full name of centre

Town

Forename(s)

Surname

Number of seat

Date of birth

Day	Month	Year	Scottish candidate number

Total marks — 90

SECTION 1 — 20 marks

Attempt ALL questions.

SECTION 2 — 70 marks

Attempt ALL questions.

Show all working.

Write your answers clearly in the spaces provided in this booklet. Additional space for answers is provided at the end of this booklet. If you use this space you must clearly identify the question number you are attempting.

Use **blue** or **black** ink.

Before leaving the examination room you must give this booklet to the Invigilator; if you do not, you may lose all the marks for this paper.

MARKS | DO NOT WRITE IN THIS MARGIN

SECTION 1 — 20 marks

Attempt ALL questions

1. Describe the difference between an internal and an external hyperlink.

    2

2. Describe how a real number is stored in a computer's memory.

    2

3. The validity of a password is checked as part of a program.

    ```
    . . .
    Line 8     SET passValid TO false
    Line 9     RECEIVE userPassword FROM (STRING) KEYBOARD
    Line10     IF userPassword = storedPassword THEN
    Line 11        SET passValid TO true
    Line 12    END IF
    . . .
    ```

    State the **data type** used to store the variable "passValid".

    1

4. Describe how vector graphics are stored in a computer.

    2

MARKS | DO NOT WRITE IN THIS MARGIN

5. A graphic of a dog is placed in front of a coloured rectangle.

State a suitable file format for the dog graphic.   1

_____

6. An example of a URL (Uniform Resource Locator) is shown below.

https://www.largebank.com/loanadvice.rtf

Identify the standard file format that would be downloaded when this URL is selected.   1

_____

7. Part of a program is shown below.

```
Line 1:     DECLARE score AS REAL INITIALLY 0·0
Line 2:     RECEIVE score FROM KEYBOARD
Line 3:     IF score > 2·0 THEN
Line 4:        SEND "Congratulations. You are in the final" TO DISPLAY
Line 5:     ELSE
Line 6:        SEND "You have failed to qualify" TO DISPLAY
Line 7:     END IF
```

Describe what happens in Lines 3 to 6 when the value 1·4 is entered at Line 2.   2

_____

_____

_____

_____

8. An example of a database record is shown below.

Employees					
Employee ID	Forename	Surname	Full Time	Home Phone Number	Mobile Phone Number
2365	Dee	Rossborough	True	01383 712345	07974 354267

(a) Explain why the Employee ID field requires a presence check.

1

(b) Employee photographs are to be added to the database record.

State a field type which should be used to contain a photograph of each employee.

1

9. State the component that enables a processor and a hard disk drive to communicate.

1

10. Some digital video cameras allow videos to be downloaded to computer systems using both a wired and wireless connection.

State one advantage of each transmission media over the other when downloading video.

2

Wired advantage _____

Wireless advantage _____

MARKS | DO NOT WRITE IN THIS MARGIN

11. State the feature of a web browser that ensures that the history of websites visited by a user are not saved.

1

_____

_____

12. A complex condition is used to decide if hotel customers qualify for a free night's stay. Part of the program is shown below.

. . .

```
Line 21    IF nightsBooked >= 6  AND (NOT (cardType = Bronze)) THEN
Line 22        SEND custName TO DISPLAY
Line 23    END IF
```

. . .

State all possible outputs when the following test data is used in this program.

2

custName	cardType	nightsBooked
J Kerr	Gold	3
P Singh	Silver	8
R Kroon	Bronze	7
H Smith	Gold	6

[Turn over

13. Part of the design of a program is shown below.

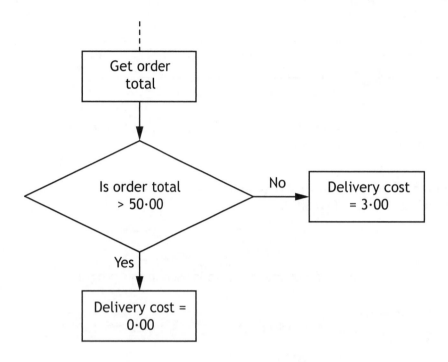

Identify the graphical design notation shown above.   **1**

_____

MARKS | DO NOT WRITE IN THIS MARGIN

SECTION 2 — 70 MARKS

Attempt ALL Questions

14. Bike Scotland uses a flat file database to store details of its members and affiliated cycling clubs.

Membership Number	Forename	Surname	Date of Birth	Club Code	Club Name	Founded	Number of Members
011-423	Alojzy	Czajka	15/03/1979	24FW05	Free Wheel	16/10/2000	67
192-033	Donny	Carruthers	20/02/1982	77SU22	Spokes United	29/04/1985	29
213-847	Salim	Hanif	09/06/1994	12DW39	District Wheelers	03/01/1954	45
624-536	Harry	Fence	01/02/1963	12DW39	District Wheelers	03/01/1954	45
018-253	Derrick	Smith	12/12/1970	77SU22	Spokes United	29/04/1985	29
773-362	Maria	Amonte	02/11/1999	24FW05	Free Wheel	16/10/2000	67
836-555	Fiona	Hewitt	20/02/1972	77SU22	Spokes United	29/04/1985	29
983-543	Samantha	Wellbeck	18/09/1975	77SU22	Spokes United	29/04/1985	29
098-133	Tracy	Uttley	30/05/2000	12DW39	District Wheelers	03/01/1954	45

(a) State the **field type** used to store each Membership Number.   1

_____

(b) The database contains personal information.

   (i) State the **Act** with which Bike Scotland must comply.   1

   _____

   _____

   (ii) Describe what Bike Scotland must do to ensure it complies with this Act when collecting this information.   1

   _____

   _____

   _____

MARKS DO NOT WRITE IN THIS MARGIN

14. **(continued)**

The database is redesigned and implemented as a relational database with two linked tables.

Cyclist

Membership Number	Forename	Surname	Date of Birth	Club Code
098-133	Tracy	Uttley	30/05/2000	12DW39
213-847	Salim	Hanif	09/06/1994	12DW39
624-536	Harry	Fence	01/02/1963	12DW39
011-423	Alojzy	Czajka	15/03/1979	24FW05
773-362	Maria	Amonte	02/11/1999	24FW05
018-253	Derrick	Smith	12/12/1970	77SU22
192-033	Donny	Carruthers	20/02/1982	77SU22
836-555	Fiona	Hewitt	20/02/1972	77SU22
983-543	Samantha	Wellbeck	18/09/1975	77SU22

Club

Club Code	Club Name	Founded	Number of Members
12DW39	District Wheelers	03/01/1954	45
24FW05	Free Wheel	16/10/2000	67
77SU22	Spokes United	29/04/1985	29

(c) Describe two advantages of using a relational database rather than a flat file database for storing the data. 2

Advantage 1 _____

_____

Advantage 2 _____

_____

MARKS | DO NOT WRITE IN THIS MARGIN

14. (continued)

(d) (i) Explain why the Club Code field is a primary key and a foreign key in the relational database.

2

_____

_____

_____

_____

(ii) When adding a new club to the Club table the following error message is displayed:

Club code **12OYB22** is invalid, please re-enter

State the validation that has been applied to the field Club Code.

1

_____

_____

(e) The Cyclist table has been sorted on two fields.

Describe how the table has been sorted.

2

_____

_____

_____

_____

_____

[Turn over

MARKS | DO NOT WRITE IN THIS MARGIN

15. A program is being developed to monitor the availability of parking spaces in a multi-level car park. The car park has three levels, each with 50 numbered spaces and a digital display board that shows the number of spaces available on each level.

Level	Numbered Spaces
Red	1–50
Black	51–100
Yellow	101–150

Part of the program is shown below:

Line 1   DECLARE redAvailable AS INTEGER INITIALLY 50
Line 2   DECLARE blackAvailable AS INTEGER INITIALLY 50
Line 3   DECLARE yellowAvailable AS INTEGER INITIALLY 50
. . .
. . .
                < vehicle is detected occupying a space>
. . .
. . .

Line 22   IF spaceNumber ≥1 AND spaceNumber ≤50 THEN
Line 23   redAvailable = redAvailable − 1
Line 24   END IF

. . .
. . .

(a) Explain why integer data types are used in Lines 1 to 3.   1

_____

_____

MARKS | DO NOT WRITE IN THIS MARGIN

15. (continued)

(b) Name the part of the computer system that will carry out each of the following tasks during the execution of Line 23.

(i) Carries the location of redAvailable in main memory.   1

_____

(ii) Transfers the value of redAvailable from main memory to the processor.   1

_____

(iii) Calculates the new value of redAvailable.   1

_____

[Turn over

15.   **(continued)**

When a vehicle parks, the digital display board will be updated to show the number of available spaces on each level.

SPACES AVAILABLE
Red Level   FULL
Black Level   8
Yellow Level   32

(c)   (i)   Complete the condition below, that will display the message "FULL" when all the spaces on the Red Level are occupied.   **1**

IF_____THEN

           SEND "FULL" TO DISPLAY

END IF

(ii)   Each of the letters of the message **FULL** will be stored as an ASCII character.

Calculate the number of bits required to store this message.   **1**

MARKS | DO NOT WRITE IN THIS MARGIN

15.   (continued)

(d) Each of the parking space numbers is stored in binary.

State the decimal equivalent of the binary number 01101100.   1

(e) While the parking space program is being developed, it is executed using an interpreter.

(i) State one advantage of using an interpreter rather than a compiler at the development stage of a program.   1

_____

_____

(ii) The finished program is compiled.

State two advantages of executing a compiled version compared to an interpreted version.   2

Advantage 1 _____

_____

_____

Advantage 2 _____

_____

_____

16. Jenny works for a website design company. Her latest project is to design and implement a website for Go Universe.

She creates the website below.

(a) Identify two features of the user interface that Jenny included to aid navigation.   **2**

Feature 1_____

_____

Feature 2_____

_____

(b) Identify one area of this website where Javascript has been used to add interactivity.   **1**

_____

_____

MARKS | DO NOT WRITE IN THIS MARGIN

16.   **(continued)**

(c)   Jenny used the simple template below when coding the HTML.

```
<!DOCTYPE html>
<html>

<head>
    <title> </title>
</head>

<body>
<div>
    <p>Page Heading</p>
</div>
</body>

</html>
```

Describe how the above HTML was edited to make the words "Go Books" appear at the top of the webpage.   **1**

_____

_____

_____

(d)

The above logo is added to each page using the following code.

`<img src="graphics/logo.bmp" alt="Logo" style="width:120px;height:60px;">`

(i)   The code contains the link to the stored graphic file.

State the type of addressing used.   **1**

_____

[Turn over

MARKS | DO NOT WRITE IN THIS MARGIN

16. (d) (continued)

(ii) The original graphic was saved with a colour depth of 24 bits.

Calculate, using appropriate units, the storage requirements of the graphic.   **3**

Show your working in the box below.

(iii) Explain why compressing the graphic would benefit the **users** of the Go Universe website.   **1**

_____

_____

_____

(e) State one test that could be carried out on the website.   **1**

_____

_____

[Turn over for next question

DO NOT WRITE ON THIS PAGE

MARKS DO NOT WRITE IN THIS MARGIN

17. An online pet supply retailer is offering a special deal to customers buying at least **two**, but not more than **six**, bags of pet food. If customers try to buy any other quantity, a message is displayed.

For example:

Input

Special Deal
Please enter the number of bags of pet food you would like to buy:

8

Output

Quantity not valid.
Please try again.

(a) Show, using pseudocode or a programming language of your choice, how input validation could be used to ensure an acceptable number of bags is entered.

4

MARKS | DO NOT WRITE IN THIS MARGIN

17. (continued)

(b) The data in the table below will be used to test the program.

Complete the table.   **2**

Type of Test Data	Test Data	Expected Results
Extreme		Proceed to next section of code
Exceptional	Three	Program cannot run! Invalid data type
	4	Proceed to next section of code

(c) When testing the program using the data from the table, "Three" is entered. As expected, an error message appears.

```
Program cannot run!
Invalid data type
```

(i) Name this type of error.   **1**

_____

(ii) Explain why this error occurred when testing the program.   **1**

_____

_____

(d) A syntax error can occur when writing code.

(i) Explain what is meant by a syntax error.   **1**

_____

_____

(ii) Explain how the editing features in software development environments can help identify syntax errors.   **1**

_____

_____

MARKS | DO NOT WRITE IN THIS MARGIN

18. Fass is an art dealer. When he visits an artist's studio, he uses a catalogue app on his mobile phone to store photographs and information about artworks he plans to sell.

(a) Fass has bought a new mobile phone.

Old Phone		New Phone	
Processor	Dual-core 2·5GHz	Processor	Quad-core 2·5GHz
Memory	1GB RAM	Memory	2GB RAM
Camera	16 Megapixel Rear 2 Megapixel Front	Camera	16 Megapixel Rear 2 Megapixel Front
Storage	32GB Solid State	Storage	32GB Solid State 1TB Free Cloud
Screen Size	1334x750 pixels	Screen Size	1920x1080 pixels
Additional Features	Biometric Security	Additional Features	Biometric Security Automatic Cloud Backup

(i) State one feature found on the new phone that may allow the catalogue app to run faster than on his old phone.

1

_____

_____

(ii) Fass uses cloud storage to store the photographs.

State one advantage and one disadvantage of cloud storage instead of his local phone storage.

2

Advantage _____

_____

Disadvantage _____

_____

MARKS DO NOT WRITE IN THIS MARGIN

18. **(continued)**

(b) Explain why Fass must ask permission to store a digital copy of the artists' artwork.

1

_____

_____

(c) Fass can record video using his new phone.

State a standard file format for storing video on his mobile phone.

1

_____

(d) State one biometric security method that would ensure that only Fass can access his mobile phone.

1

_____

(e) While visiting an artist's studio, Fass asks permission to use the studio's wireless network.

State the Act that Fass would have broken if he had used the wireless network without permission.

1

_____

(f) Fass is given a free laptop computer with his new phone.

(i) State one advantage of the phone's solid state storage compared to the magnetic hard disk drive in the laptop.

1

_____

_____

(ii) Fass sends his old phone for disposal.

Describe how the correct disposal of his old phone reduces environmental impact.

2

_____

_____

_____

_____

_____

19. Louise is conducting a survey at her school to find out how many hours per week her class mates spend playing computer games. Louise will survey 100 pupils.

The program assigns 100 names to a 1-D array as shown below.

Line 1   DECLARE name AS ARRAY OF STRING INITIALLY []
Line 2   RECEIVE name[0] FROM KEYBOARD
Line 3   RECEIVE name[1] FROM KEYBOARD
Line 4   RECEIVE name[2] FROM KEYBOARD
. . .
. . .
Line 101   RECEIVE name[99] FROM KEYBOARD

(a) Louise realises that writing the code to read the data into the array like this is time consuming and not good practice.

Write, using pseudocode or a programming language of your choice, the code to show how the data can be entered into the 1-D array using repetition.

3

MARKS | DO NOT WRITE IN THIS MARGIN

19. (continued)

(b) Another section of the program is shown below.

```
. . .
Line 119    SET averageHours = totalHours / 7
Line 120    <use a pre-defined function to store averageHours to the
            nearest whole number>
Line 121    SEND "An average of " & averageHours & " hours" TO
            DISPLAY
```

(i) Identify the operator used to concatenate in the program above.   1

_____

(ii) Explain why averageHours should be stored as a real data type.   1

_____

_____

(iii) The program is executed. At Line 119 the value 4·26 is assigned to averageHours.

Write the message that will be displayed when Line 121 is executed.   2

(iv) State the pre-defined function that could be used when Line 120 is coded.   1

_____

[Turn over

MARKS | DO NOT WRITE IN THIS MARGIN

19. (continued)

(c) Louise gives a copy of her finished program to her friend who tells her that the program code is difficult to read.

(i) Explain how indentation can help readability in the program.   **1**

_____

_____

_____

(ii) State one other programming technique used to improve readability of programs.   **1**

_____

[Turn over for next question

DO NOT WRITE ON THIS PAGE

MARKS | DO NOT WRITE IN THIS MARGIN

20. Sea Otter Observations uses a simple website to provide information about otters. The home page for the website is shown below.

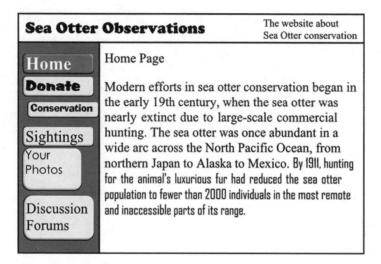

(a) Identify two examples of poor consistency in the user interface above.   2

Example 1 _____

_____

Example 2 _____

_____

(b) A high quality sound file of otters communicating with each other is edited for the website. The sound quality of the edited file is poor.

Describe one factor that has affected the quality of this sound.   1

_____

_____

_____

MARKS | DO NOT WRITE IN THIS MARGIN

20. (continued)

(c) When a user clicks on the 'Your Photos' button on the home page, they are directed to the page below.

(i) State two network hardware devices required to connect to the Internet to access the website.   **2**

Device 1 _____

Device 2 _____

(ii) State the feature of a browser that would enable a user to view a close-up of the otters' whiskers.   **1**

_____

(d) Draw, referring to the home page and the other pages as examples, a diagram to represent the navigation structure of the Sea Otter Observations website.   **2**

MARKS DO NOT WRITE IN THIS MARGIN

20. **(continued)**

(e) A hacker alters a link from the home page. The altered link now directs the user to the hacker's version of the donations page shown below.

Hacker's Version

Sea Oter Observatins

The website about
Sea Otter conservation

Donate

Donations

If u would like to donat to the otters please enter you bank details below to log into your bank account and give us money.

Name
Date of Birth
Name of Bank
Account Number
Sort Code
Password

Official

Sea Otter Observations

The website about
Sea Otter conservation

Donate

Home

Donations

If you would like to donate money to the conservation of sea otters, please click on the secure link below.

Make Secure Payment

(i) Explain why the hacker's version is an example of phishing. 1

_____

_____

(ii) Identify one item on the hacker's version that could make the user suspect that it is not genuine. 1

_____

_____

[END OF QUESTION PAPER]

ADDITIONAL SPACE FOR ANSWERS

ADDITIONAL SPACE FOR ANSWERS

NATIONAL 5

2017 Specimen Question Paper

N5

National Qualifications
SPECIMEN ONLY

Mark

S816/75/01

Computing Science

Date — Not applicable

Duration — 2 hours

Fill in these boxes and read what is printed below.

Full name of centre

Town

Forename(s)

Surname

Number of seat

Date of birth

Day	Month	Year		Scottish candidate number

Total marks — 110

SECTION 1 — 25 marks

Attempt ALL questions.

SECTION 2 — 85 marks

Attempt ALL questions.

Write your answers clearly in the spaces provided in this booklet. Additional space for answers is provided at the end of this booklet. If you use this space you must clearly identify the question number you are attempting.

Use **blue** or **black** ink.

Before leaving the examination room you must give this booklet to the Invigilator; if you do not, you may lose all the marks for this paper.

SQA

MARKS | DO NOT WRITE IN THIS MARGIN

SECTION 1 — 25 marks

Attempt ALL questions

1. Convert the following 8-bit binary number into denary.   1

   1011 0111

2. Explain why it may be necessary to return to the implementation stage of an iterative development process after the testing stage.   1

   _____

   _____

   _____

3. State two implications of the Data Protection Act for a business that stores the personal details of its staff.   2

   Implication 1_____

   _____

   Implication 2_____

   _____

MARKS | DO NOT WRITE IN THIS MARGIN

4. The code below monitors the speed of a vehicle:

. . .

Line 5   `RECEIVE speed FROM <sensor>`

Line 6   `WHILE speed <= 70 DO`

Line 7   `RECEIVE speed FROM <sensor>`

Line 8   `END WHILE`

Line 9   `SEND signal TO <alarm>`

Describe what happens in lines 6 to 9 above if the sensor detects a value of 83 at line 5.   **3**

_____

_____

_____

_____

5. The Bank of Aberdeen uses a firewall and encryption to ensure data is kept secure.

(a) Explain the purpose of a firewall.   **1**

_____

_____

(b) Explain how encryption can keep data secure.   **1**

_____

_____

6. An ASCII character set contains both control characters and printable characters.

State one example of each.   **2**

Control character_____

Printable character_____

MARKS | DO NOT WRITE IN THIS MARGIN

7. Explain why web designers make use of low-fidelity prototyping.

1

_____

_____

_____

8. A vector graphic file stores objects and their attributes.

(a) State the name of the object shown above.

1

_____

(b) State two attributes of this object.

2

Attribute 1 _____

Attribute 2 _____

9. A pottery shop's database allows users to choose a type of plate, as follows:

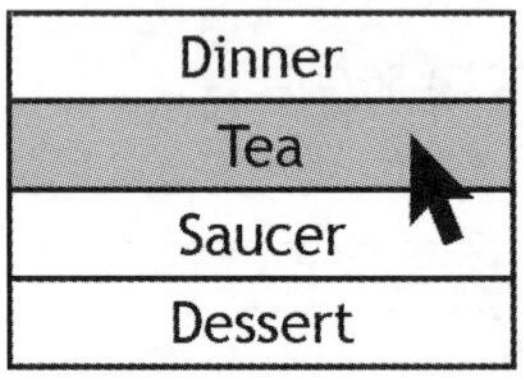

Dinner
Tea
Saucer
Dessert

(a) State the type of validation shown above.

1

_____

(b) Describe why the database uses this type of validation.

1

_____

_____

MARKS | DO NOT WRITE IN THIS MARGIN

10. Jane is entering an online competition. She edits a recording of herself singing to save and upload to the competition's website.

Describe one advantage and one disadvantage of saving and uploading an MP3 file format rather than a WAV file format to the website.   **2**

Advantage of MP3 file format_____

_____

Disadvantage of MP3 file format_____

_____

11. Switching off a computer system when it is not being used reduces energy use.

Describe two other methods of reducing the energy use of a computer system.   **2**

Method 1 _____

_____

Method 2 _____

_____

12. The value 195 would be stored in a computer system using 'floating-point representation' as shown below:

$$0{\cdot}195 \times 10^3$$

Identify the mantissa and exponent in the above floating-point representation.   **2**

Mantissa _____

Exponent _____

13. A web page can use both internal and external hyperlinks.

Explain the difference between an internal and an external hyperlink.   **2**

_____

_____

_____

_____

_____

SECTION 2 — 85 marks

Attempt ALL questions

14. Mark writes a program to calculate a worker's average weekly wage.

The first part of the program asks the user to log in. They are given three attempts to enter the correct password which is 'Bingo'.

. . .

```
Line 6   SET attempts TO 0
Line 7   REPEAT
Line 8      RECEIVE password FROM KEYBOARD
Line 9      SET attempts TO attempts +1
Line 10  UNTIL _____
```

. . .

(a) Complete line 10 of the code above.   3

(b) State the data type of the variable `password`.   1

_____

The following section of code calculates the average weekly wage:

```
Line 11  RECEIVE day1 FROM KEYBOARD
Line 12  RECEIVE day2 FROM KEYBOARD
Line 13  RECEIVE day3 FROM KEYBOARD
Line 14  RECEIVE day4 FROM KEYBOARD
Line 15  RECEIVE day5 FROM KEYBOARD
Line 16  RECEIVE day6 FROM KEYBOARD
Line 17  RECEIVE day7 FROM KEYBOARD
Line 18  SET weeklyAverage TO (day1 + day2 + day3 + day4 +
         day5 + day6 + day7)/7
Line 19  <display the seven days wages and average>
```

MARKS | DO NOT WRITE IN THIS MARGIN

14. (continued)

(c) When evaluating this code, it is found to be inefficient.

Using a programming language of your choice, rewrite lines 11 to 18 of the code using more efficient constructs.

5

[Turn over

15. Two golfers from a golf club are in the headline article of the 'Scotland Yesterday' newspaper.

(a) The golf club wishes to add a new web page to the club's website, which will include:

- information from the newspaper article

- photographs of the golfers

- a video interview with the golfers.

Using this information, draw a wireframe design for the new page.   3

MARKS | DO NOT WRITE IN THIS MARGIN

15.   (continued)

(b)   A cascading style sheet (CSS) rule shown below is used to style the large headings in the golf club's website:

```
h1 { font-size: 20px;

     font-family: "Times New Roman";

     text-align: center;

}
```

Paragraph text in this website should be displayed on the left, using a Helvetica font that is half the height of the text used in the large headings.

Write a CSS rule that would style the paragraphs.   **4**

(c)   The golf club's website is tested by club members. Two members report that the video does not display correctly.

Describe two additional tests that could be performed on the website.   **2**

Test 1 _____

_____

Test 2 _____

_____

[Turn over

16. Pam is creating an application that will find and display a person's tax rate based on their salary.

Salary	Tax rate
0–12000	0
12001–40000	20
40001 upwards	40

(a) Analyse the problem and identify the input, the process and the output.   3

Input _____

Process _____

Output _____

(b) Using a design technique of your choice, design an efficient solution to the problem of finding a person's tax rate.   4

17. Angela works in a cycle shop. She decides to create a database to store information on staff and bikes. This would make it easier to record which staff member prepared each bike for sale.

Angela starts by analysing the problem. She looks at what information the store currently holds on paper and makes notes as follows:

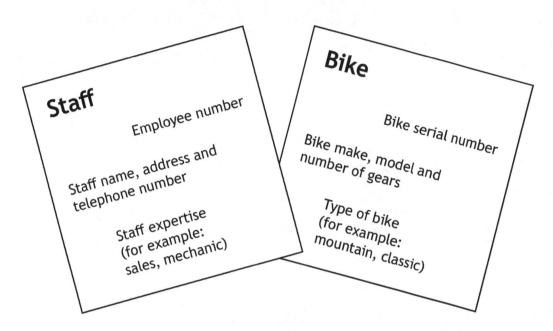

(a) Complete the entity-relationship diagram below.   4

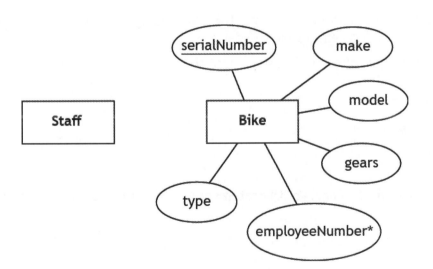

[Turn over

Page eleven

17.   **(continued)**

(b) Following implementation of the database, the 'Bike' table below contains 11 records.

serialNumber	make	model	type	gears	employeeNumber
20X5346F	Boardman	CX Team 14	Road	20	11
RAL09787	Raleigh	Cameo	Classic	7	9
RAL026356	Raleigh	Cuckoo	Classic	3	9
863345467	Carrera	Kraken	Mountain	27	10
20X62983	Boardman	MB Comp	Mountain	20	7
V0973647	Voodoo	Malice	BMX	1	7
30X6253J	Boardman	Team	Hybrid	21	9
V02377643	Voodoo	Malice	BMX	1	7
RAL97436	Raleigh	Cameo	Classic	7	12
RAL09944	Raleigh	Sprint	Road	21	11
30X76543	Boardman	CX Team 14	Road	20	11

Angela notices data entry errors. The two Raleigh Cameo bikes have 8 gears and not 7 as entered in the database.

She writes the following SQL statement to correct these errors.

```
UPDATE Bike
SET gears = 7
WHERE make = "Raleigh";
```

(i) Explain why Angela's SQL statement **would not** correct these errors.   1

_____

_____

(ii) Explain why Angela's SQL statement would create additional errors in the database.   1

_____

_____

MARKS DO NOT WRITE IN THIS MARGIN

17. (continued)

(c) Angela wishes to remove the following bike from the database.

Serial Number: 30X76543

Make: Boardman

Model: CX Team 14

Type: Road

Gears: 20

(i) Evaluate the effect of running the SQL statement below: 2

```
DELETE FROM Bike
WHERE make = "Boardman" AND model = "CX Team 14";
```

(ii) Describe a better solution Angela could use to remove the bike from the database.   1

[Turn over

18. John has created a website listing his favourite things. The home page of his website is shown below.

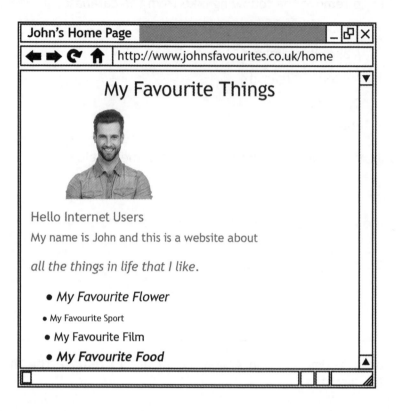

(a) John tests his website using a browser and notices a lack of consistency.
Explain why John's home page lacks consistency.   2

_____

_____

_____

_____

MARKS | DO NOT WRITE IN THIS MARGIN

18.   (continued)

(b) John wishes to show his favourite sports as a bullet point list on his 'favourite sports' page. His list of favourite sports will be implemented using <ul> and <li> tags.

Add HTML <ul> and <li> opening and closing tags to the list below.

3

Golf

Cricket

Ten Pin Bowling

[Turn over

18. **(continued)**

One of John's linked pages shows his favourite flower. When the HTML document below is displayed in a browser, it generates the web page shown.

HTML document

```
<!DOCTYPE html>
<html>
<head>
<title>Page Title</title>
<style>
h1 {font-size:20px;font-style:bold;text-align:center}
p {font-size:12px;color:DarkGreen;text-align:left}
#latin {font-size:10px;font-style:italic;color:LightGreen}
img {width:304px;height:300px;align-left}
</style>
</head>

<body>
<h1>My Favourite Flower</h1>

<p>My favourite flower is called a Magnolia. They are ancient flowers thought
to be around 20 million years old. A picture of a Magnolia in full flower is
shown below.<br>

<img id="photo" src="magnolia.jpg" alt="Magnolia Flower"
onmouseover="document.getElementById('photo').src='magnoliaFlower.jpg'"/>
</p>

<p ID="latin">Magnolioideae</p>

</body>
</html>
```

Web page

My Favourite Flower

My favourite flower is called a Magnolia. They are ancient flowers thought to be around 20 million years old. A picture of a Magnolia in full flower is shown below.

Magnolioideae

18. (continued)

   (c) The <img> tag contains some additional code used to create dynamic content.

      (i) State the language used to create dynamic content in web pages.   **1**

_____

      (ii) The graphic changes when the mouse pointer is placed over it.

           Identify the event in the code that causes the graphic to change.   **1**

_____

   (d) The text in the web page uses internal style rules positioned in the <head>.

      (i) State the type of CSS selector shown by the # symbol at the beginning of the CSS rule below.   **1**

```
#latin {font-size:10px;font-style:italic;color:LightGreen;}
```

_____

      (ii) The CSS rules below contain three styles each.

```
p {font-size:12px; color:DarkGreen; text-align:left}
#latin {font-size:10px; font-style:italic; color:LightGreen;}
```

           Both of these rules have been applied to the text below the graphic.

```
p ID="latin">Magnolioideae</p>
```

           Describe how the text below the graphic will look when it is viewed in a browser.   **3**

_____

_____

_____

[Turn over

18. **(continued)**

(e) The favourite flower page includes an image tag linked to a bit-mapped graphic.

`src="magnolia.jpg"`

   (i) Describe how a bit-mapped graphic is represented in a computer system's memory.

   2

   _____

   _____

   (ii) State why the file type of the bit-mapped graphic is suitable for use on a web page.

   2

   _____

   _____

(f) John is advised to use an external cascading style sheet.

Describe what is meant by an external cascading style sheet.

2

_____

_____

_____

(g) John used a search engine to find a suitable graphic to use on each of his pages.

State one way John could ensure he does not breach the Copyright, Designs and Patents Act 1988.

1

_____

MARKS | DO NOT WRITE IN THIS MARGIN

19. Read the following design for a solution to a problem.

Algorithm

1   Ask the user to enter their name

2   Ask the user to enter their flight details

3   Generate the holiday booking reference

4   Display the holiday booking reference

Refinements

1.1 Ask user to enter surname only

2.1 Ask user to enter first three letters of departure airport (for example: Edi for Edinburgh)

2.2 Ask user to enter first three letters of arrival airport

3.1 Store the booking reference as: arrival airport string + surname + departure airport string

(a) State which design technique has been used for the above solution.   **1**

_____

(b) State the output expected if the design is tested by Kate Bryant who is flying from Glasgow to Barcelona.   **3**

_____

(c) Refinement 3.1 stores the holiday booking reference.

State two programming constructs that would be required to implement this refinement.   **2**

Construct 1_____

Construct 2_____

(d) When implementing the above solution, describe one advantage of using an interpreter and one advantage of using a compiler to translate the program code into binary.   **2**

Interpreter_____

_____

Compiler_____

_____

19. **(continued)**

(e) Using a design technique of your choice, add input validation to refinement 2.1 to ensure that the user only enters a 3 character string. An error message should inform the user when their input is not valid.

4

20. Scot Cars (a second-hand car company) has branches located in five different Scottish towns and cities. They maintain a database of all cars they have in stock. Some of the records from the relational database are shown below.

Table name: Branch				
branchNumber	street	town	postcode	dateFounded
18536423	10 Glasgow Road	Hamilton	HA9 8FR	14/07/1962
29736453	13 Pretty Drive	Inverness	IN2 13GW	11/12/1970
99108663	194 Collinton Avenue	Edinburgh	EH28 1PK	28/02/1965
36352363	125 Milk Way	Glasgow	G2 3HJ	17/01/2010
28635491	243 Bents Road	Dundee	DN14 7CD	01/10/1997

Table name: Car							
make	model	colour	registration	mileage	electricWindows	alloyWheels	branchNumber
Ford	Ka	White	SL23 GTD	37970	Yes	No	99108663
Volkswagen	Golf	Black	ST99 FDT	33200	Yes	Yes	18536423
Ford	Escort	Silver	X364 TNK	120665	No	No	28635491
Vauxhall	Corsa	Yellow	BH20 SWZ	4009	Yes	Yes	28635491
Nissan	Qashqai	Black	SH88 NNG	67118	Yes	Yes	18536423
BMW	3 Series	Blue	SH34 BNM	33200	Yes	Yes	29736453
Ford	Ka	Green	SL85 HDF	40029	No	No	29736453

MARKS

(a) Scot Car's relational database contains primary and foreign keys.

(i) State the purpose of a foreign key in a relational database. 1

_____

[Turn over

MARKS | DO NOT WRITE IN THIS MARGIN

20. (a) (continued)

(ii) Complete the table below to identify the keys that were created when this relational database was implemented.   **3**

	Table	Field
Primary key		
Primary key		
Foreign key		

(iii) State the relationship that exists between the two implemented tables.   **1**

_____

(b) State the output from the following SQL statement.   **3**

```
SELECT make, model, registration
FROM Car
WHERE colour="Black"
ORDER BY make ASC;
```

MARKS | DO NOT WRITE IN THIS MARGIN

20.   (continued)

(c)   Customers often visit Scot Cars looking for a particular make and model of car.

Design a search that would provide customers with an ordered list of cars, as shown below.

4

Model	Colour	Town	Mileage
Ka	White	Edinburgh	37970
Ka	Silver	Glasgow	38002
Ka	Green	Inverness	40029
Ka	Black	Dundee	43099
Ka	Green	Hamilton	50103
Ka	White	Edinburgh	52086
Ka	Brown	Edinburgh	78192

Field(s)	
Table(s)	
Search criteria	
Sort order	

[Turn over

21. Arthur's Antiques sells old furniture. All staff receive a monthly bonus of £50, which is increased if they sell over 10 items of furniture. The bonus is increased further if they sell over 20 items of furniture.

A design for the program used to calculate the bonus payment for each of the four members of staff is shown below.

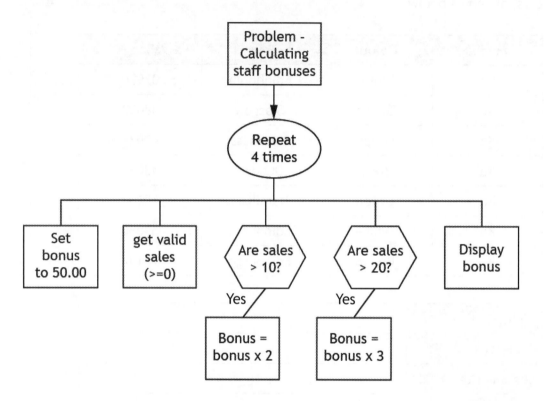

(a) List the variables and data types that would be required to implement the design.

The first one has been completed for you. **2**

Variable name	Data type
loop	integer

(b) The program is implemented to match the design.

State examples of exceptional and extreme test data that could be used when inputting staff sales. **2**

Exceptional _____

Extreme _____

MARKS | DO NOT WRITE IN THIS MARGIN

21. (continued)

(c) The program is further tested with normal test data. The results are shown below.

	Sales input	Expected output	Actual output
Staff 1	6	Bonus is 50	Bonus is 50
Staff 2	10	Bonus is 50	Bonus is 50
Staff 3	15	Bonus is 100	Bonus is 100
Staff 4	22	Bonus is 150	**Bonus is 300**

The test data for Staff 4 shows there is an error in the design.

(i) State the type of error.   1

_____

(ii) Describe how this design error could be corrected. You may wish to write a description or re-draw part of the design.   2

MARKS DO NOT WRITE IN THIS MARGIN

21. **(continued)**

(d) When the program is running it carries out the following tasks:

- stores the original bonus value of 50

- checks if sales > 10

(i) State the part of the processor that would temporarily store the value 50.

1

_____

(ii) State the part of the processor that would compare the sales value to the value 10.

1

_____

[END OF SPECIMEN QUESTION PAPER]

ADDITIONAL SPACE FOR ANSWERS AND ROUGH WORK

ADDITIONAL SPACE FOR ANSWERS AND ROUGH WORK

NATIONAL 5 COMPUTING SCIENCE 2016

1. 1 1 1 0 0 0 1 1

2. Easier to edit/maintain.
or
Another programmer can understand the code.

3. The database cannot be edited.

4. *Any one from:*
- No typing error/human error
- Only one can be selected
- Limits possible inputs
- Appropriate input when no keyboard, for example touchscreen device

5. To store data temporarily.

6. *Any two from:*
- Firewall
- Spam killer
- Spyware protection
- Malware protection (Trojan)
- Biometric (software)
- Email protection
- Parental control
- Privacy
- Phishing protection
- Encryption (software)
- Password manager
- Backup
- Social network protection

7.
- Phishing
- Malware/spyware
- Hacking
- Virus
- Trojan

8. Expert

9. *All three bullets for 2 marks:*
- Program loops/program repeats lines 3 and 4/program checks condition
- A message is displayed
- Another temperature reading is taken

Any two bullets for 1 mark.
One or **zero** bullets: no marks.

10. Search **or** Query

11. 1. Compiler (1)
2. Interpreter (1)

12. *1 mark each for:*
- Loop 16 times
- Input of time from user inside loop

13. *Description of two problems and improvements from poor navigation list below:*
- Navigation in two different places
- Navigation not labelled correctly (buttons along top, 'radio buttons', 'check boxes', 'new' button, 'arrow' button)
- No indication of which page (1,2,3,4,5) the user is currently on
- No indication where login will take you

1 mark for each problem and improvement required.
If candidate states two problems without improvements award **1** mark.

14. Peer to Peer **or** P2P

15. (a) *Any one from:*
- Route ID data value is not unique
- Cannot identify one row in the table using Route ID data value

(b) *Any two problems from:*
- Data duplication
- Inconsistency of data
- Update anomalies

(c) Relational (database)
or
Linked (tables)

(d) Text

(e) (i) *Any one from:*
- Restricted (choice)
- Presence check

(ii) Exceptional (1 mark):
- Any value less than 1 or
- Any value greater than 6 or
- And real value
- Any example of text value

Extreme (1 mark):
- 1
or
- 6

(f) *Two fields in correct order with sorting direction:*
- Price ascending
- Depart ascending

16. (a) *Design or code should include the following bullet points for 1 mark each:*
- Loop
- Loop condition
- User input, numTwo re-entered after condition (or within loop...until)
- Error message to user

(b) Character (char)

(c) Output would be:
"Correct it is in the middle"

(d) *1 mark for each:*
- Random (Number)
- To generate a random value between two values
or
- Between a range
or
- Between limits

(e) Lines 3 to 17 (or 3 to 18) should be placed inside a loop (1 mark)
Repeat 10 times (1 mark)

17. (a) Hierarchical

(b) *Description or naming of:*
- Storyboard
- Wireframe

(c) *Description of function of hyperlink:*
- Provides navigation through a website
- Click on hyperlink to move to another resource (page)

(d) (i) Video
(ii) Looking for path and filename
resources/dunk.gif

(e) (i) (Hyper)link to another website

(ii) Uniform Resource Locator

(iii) Calculating Resolution (1 mark) 7x600x5x600
Multiplying by Colour depth (1 mark)
(12600000x24)
Convert to Megabytes (1 mark)
/8/1024/1024 = 36.048 Megabytes

18. (a) (i) Increase file size

(ii) mp3
Alternative compressed audio formats are
acceptable (but not mp4 as this is a container file
for storing video)

(b) (i) Hacking
or
Unauthorised access

(ii) *Description of one other offence under CMA:*
- Unauthorised access with intent to commit
crime/further offences
- Unauthorised modification of data

(c) Communications Act

(d) (i) Graphics are owned by someone else
or
Without permission he would break the
Copyright, Designs & patents Act

(ii) *Selection construct with appropriate condition
(1 mark):*
- IF answer = A
- IF answer = correct answer
- IF question 3 = A
Assignment to update totalscore variable (1 mark):
- totalscore TO totalscore + 1
- add one to score
- totalscore = + 1

(e) *Any two for 1 mark each:*
- Right to view own personal data
- Right to have own data corrected if incorrect
- Right to seek compensation for damages caused by
inaccurate information
- Right to prevent data being used for direct
marketing
- Right to ask for data to be deleted (if it breaches
the DPA principles)

19. (a) Array (1 mark)
Of Real (1 mark)

(b) (i) *Description includes reference to:*
- Line 1 – total set to 0
- Line 3 – loop
- Line 4 – each cost is added to previous total

(ii) Mantissa (1 mark)
Exponent (1 mark)

(iii) Error in question code
A
*Accept any answer that would have explained
the total being incorrect:*
- Logic error
- Syntax error (DUE)
- Not recompiled code
- Program not saved before being re-run
- Program only calculates 5 costs
- Program has not been run
- Has not added on the 45.00
- Line 3 has not been implemented correctly
B
1 mark for stating how error could be corrected

(c) Used to join text and variables together
or
Output includes both text and variables together
or
Used to join strings

20. (a) Blocks attempts to access a device
or
Filters incoming traffic

(b) Encryption encodes a file (1) so that it is unreadable
(1) by others

(c) (i) *Any Input device from:*
- Touch screen
- Digital camera
- Microphone
Any Output device from:
- (HD) display
- Speakers

(ii) *Any Interface type device from:*
- USB (3)
- (Micro) HDMI
- Headphone jack

(iii) *Any one for 1 mark from:*
- Temporary storage of data
- Handling of status signals
- Data conversion – serial to parallel
- Voltage conversion
- Communication between devices

(iv) *Two reasons for incompatibility (1 mark each):*
- OS version too old (4.1 needs 4.4 or higher)
- Lack of storage(16 Gigabyte needs 32 Gigabyte)

(d) *One reason that describes difference in interaction
between user and device:*
- Smartphone screen size much smaller so less room
for text and menus to be displayed
- Input device used to make selection is touch
screen so need larger icons and text than can be
selected using touch input
- Smartphone interface has fewer objects allowing
for faster download to portable device

21. (a) (i) *Any one from:*
- Provides a visual representation which can be
easier to understand
- Illustrates flow of data/sequence of processes

(ii) Input validation

(b) IF/while (1 mark)
numPlayers <=4 (1 mark)
numGames <=3 (1 mark)
or
numPlayers <5 (1 mark)
numGames <4 (1 mark)

(c) (i)

Test data type	Expected result
Normal	Booking accepted
Extreme	Booking accepted
Exceptional	**Not valid number of players**

(ii) Run time/Execution error

(d) *Any one from:*
- Internal commentary
- Meaningful identifiers
- Indentation/white space
- Highlight keywords
- Modular code

NATIONAL 5 COMPUTING SCIENCE 2017

1. Internal: links to another location within the same website (or domain)/web page (1)
   External: links to another website (or domain) (1)

2. Mantissa (1)
   Exponent (1)

3. Boolean

4. Object/shape (1)
   1 mark for:
   Stored as a set of definitions/properties/instructions/attributes
   or
   Example of at least two attributes

5. png
   gif

6. rtf
   rich text format

7. 1.4/score/value is less than 2 (1)
   Failed to qualify message is displayed or line 6 is executed (1)

8. (a) Every employee must have an ID
   (b) Graphic

9. Interface

10. Wired: speed of data transfer is greater/increased security/less interference/improved stability (1)
    Wireless: (explanation of) portability/no untidy or dangerous wires (1)

11. Privacy mode settings or suitable description (private browsing, incognito browsing etc.)

12. P Singh
    H Smith

13. Flowchart/Flow Diagram

14. (a) Text
    (b) (i) Data protection (Act)
        (ii) Must collect only relevant data
             or
             Must only collect data for the purpose they have declared
    (c) Removes data duplication (1)
        Eliminates insert/delete/update anomalies or eliminates data inconsistences (1)
    (d) (i) In one table (club) it is unique/is a unique identifier (1)
            In the other table (cyclist) it is used to link/form a relationship between the two tables (1)
        (ii) Length check
             or
             Check that it is 6 characters long
    (e) ClubCode ascending (1)
        Membership Number ascending (1)

15. (a) Only whole numbers can be accepted (can't have part of a parking space)
    (b) (i) Address Bus
        (ii) Data Bus
        (iii) Arithmetic Logic Unit (ALU)
    (c) (i) redAvailable = 0
            or
            redAvailable < 1
        (ii) 28

    (d) 108
    (e) (i) *Any one from the following:*
            • No need to leave the programming environment
            • Tracing facilities
            • Debugging facilities
            • Executes until error found allowing for easy identification of errors (1 mark each)
        (ii) Executes/runs faster (1)
             Doesn't need translator in memory (1)

16. (a) *Any two from the following features:*
        • Search (Bar)
        • Navigation bar visible at top of page
        • Breadcrumb (1 mark each)
    (b) *Any one from the following:*
        • Search button
        • Login
        • Sort By/Drop down menu
        • Selection boxes on left
        • Cart
    (c) Inserted between the title tags
    (d) (i) Relative
        (ii) 120 * 60 (1 mark) * 24 (1 mark) = 21·09KB (1 mark for correct division)
        (iii) Transfer speed increased
    (e) *Any one from the following:*
        • Test hyperlinks work
        • Test layout
        • Media displays correctly/appropriately
        • Test scripts
        • User accessibility
        • Browser compatibility

17. (a) (Conditional) loop (1)
        Correct loop condition (1)
        Input inside loop (1)
        Display error message (1)
    (b) 2 and/or 6 (1)
        Normal (1)
    (c) (i) Execution (Runtime)
        (ii) Data type expected is number (integer); data entered is string
    (d) (i) When a mistake is made in the program code.
            or
            When the rules of the programming language are broken.
        (ii) *Any one from the following:*
             • Syntax highlighting
             • Colour coded variable names
             • Automatic indentation
             • Bookmarking/flags errors
             • Comments on errors

18. (a) (i) (Quad core) processor
        (ii) *Any one from the following — **ONE** advantage and **ONE** disadvantage:*

             Advantages:
             • Capacity
             • Accessed from anywhere with internet connection
             • Files accessible from another device
             • Backup of data

             Disadvantages:
             • Relies on internet connection
             • Vulnerable to unauthorised access

(b) Copyright

(c) mp4

   or

   avi

(d) *Any one from the following:*
   - Fingerprint (Recognition/Scan)
   - Retina/Iris/Sclera (Recognition/Scan)
   - Face (Recognition/Scan)
   - Palm Prints/Veins/Geometry (Recognition/Scan)
   - Voice (Recognition)

(e) Communication (Act)

(f) (i) More robust/no moving parts
       or
       Faster access time

   (ii) Any **two** from the following:
      - Recycle components
      - Properly dispose of dangerous elements
      - Re-use by others (selling it on) (1 mark each)

19. (a) Fixed loop 100 repetitions (1)
       Correct Input (1)
       Assignment to array (1)

   (b) (i) &
          or
          ampersand

      (ii) averageHours may require a decimal point
          or
          Division may result in a real number

      (iii) An average of 4 hours
           rounding of 4·26 to 4 (1)
           correct concatenation (1)

      (iv) Round

   (c) (i) Can show clearly where one construct starts and finishes

      (ii) *Any one from:*
         - Internal commentary
         - White space
         - Meaningful identifiers (1 mark each)

20. (a) *Any two from the following:*
       - Buttons are different sizes
       - Font changes throughout
       - Text size changes throughout
       - Text style changes throughout
       - Buttons are not aligned (1 mark each)

   (b) *Any one from the following:*
      - Sampling rate too low
      - Frequency rate too low
      - Sample depth too low

   (c) (i) Network Interface Card (1)
          Router (1)

      (ii) Page zooming/zoom/magnify

   (d) Home page (1)
       Five other named pages clearly shown as sub-pages of the home page (1)

   (e) (i) (Illegal) collection of personal details/sensitive information

      (ii) *Any one from the following:*
         - Spelling or grammar errors
         - No Home button
         - Link to bank accounts
         - Request to sign in to bank accounts
         - Asked to provide password

NATIONAL 5 COMPUTING SCIENCE 2017 SPECIMEN QUESTION PAPER

1. 183

2. To correct errors

   or

   To add additional code

3. *Any two from:*
   - Data must be kept accurate
   - Data must be safe and secure
   - Data can only be used for specifically stated purposes

4. *1 mark each for:*
   - compares 83 to 70
   - doesn't enter loop (because condition is false)
   - sends signal to alarm

5. (a) Restricts access to a network

   (b) Data is coded/unreadable

6. *1 mark each for:*
   - control character example
   - printable character example

   Example responses for 6:
   - 'Start of Text', 'Escape', 'Delete' or any other character from 0-13 of ASCII code
   - A-Z, a-z, 0-9, punctuation or any visible character

7. *Either one from:*
   - To show the intended user interface to client
   - It allows end-users to get the look and feel of a website

8. (a) Ellipse

   (b) *Any two from:*
      - Co-ordinates
      - Fill colour
      - Line colour

9. (a) Restricted choice

   (b) *Either one from:*
      - Eliminates input errors
      - Users are presented with the only options

10. *One advantage from:*
    - MP3 file takes up less memory
    - MP3 file can be uploaded quickly

    One disadvantage:
    Sound quality poorer

11. *Any two from:*
    - Set computers to go into sleep mode after a period of inactivity
    - Reduce monitor settings
    - Activate hard disk shut down settings

12. Mantissa — 195
    Exponent — 3

13. *1 mark each for:*
    - Internal hyperlink — links to a page within the same website/domain
    - External hyperlink — links to page/document in another website/domain

14. (a) Password = 'Bingo' OR attempts = 3

    1 mark each for:
    - Password = 'Bingo'
    or
    - Attempts = 3

(b) String

(c) FOR eachDay FROM 1 TO 7 DO
    RECEIVE wage[eachDay] FROM KEYBOARD
    SET totalWage TO totalWage + wage[eachday]
END FOR
SET weeklyAverage TO totalWage/7

1 mark each for:
- Fixed loop
- Input
- Running total
- Divide by 7 for average outside loop
- Use of array

15. (a) *1 mark each for:*
- A picture of the two golfers (with file type)
- Text about the golf competition
- A video of the interview (with file type)

(b) *Marks awarded as noted below:*

p (1) { font-size: 10px; (1)
    font-family: "Helvetica"; (1)
    text-align: left; (1)
}

(c) *Any two from:*
- Links work
- Graphic/text display correctly
- Styling is correct
- Consistency across pages

16. (a) *1 mark each for:*
- Input — salary
- Process — decide which tax rate based on salary
- Output — tax rate

(b) *1 mark each for:*
- Selection constructs
- Conditions correct
- Tax rate assigned
- Efficient solution

Expected flowchart response for 16(b):

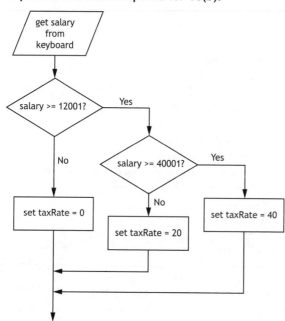

Alternative flowchart response for 16(b):

This solution would not be awarded the mark for an efficient solution.

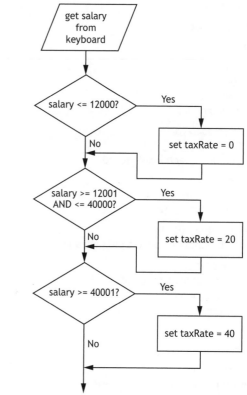

17. (a)

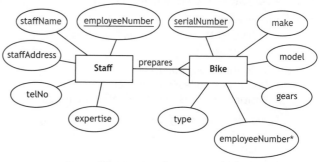

1 mark each for:
- One-to-many relationship drawn
- Relationship described
- Attributes for staff drawn
- Primary key noted

(b) (i) Gears have not been changed to 8

    (ii) All Raleigh bikes now have seven gears

(c) (i) *1 mark each for:*
- Not fit for purpose
- two records deleted (both "Boardman CX Team 14" bikes deleted)

    (ii) If delete includes the serial number

18. (a) *Any two from:*
- Text changes appearance in middle of sentence (changes to italics)
- Bullets are different sizes
- Text in bullet list in different fonts
- Text in bullet list changes styles

(b) <ul>
    <li>Golf</li>
    <li>Cricket</li>
    <li>Ten Pin Bowling</li>
    </ul>

1 mark each for:
- <ul> and </ul> surround text
- <li> and </li> surround list
- one <li></li> for each list item

(c) (i) Javascript

  (ii) Onmouseover

(d) (i) ID

  (ii) *1 mark each for:*
    • 10px
    • LightGreen
    • Italic and left

(e) (i) *1 mark each for:*
    • Grid of pixels
    • Colour of each pixel stored

  (ii) *1 mark each for:*
    • Compressed file format
    • Downloads faster

(f) Single file of styles (1)
   That can be applied to multiple pages (1)

(g) *Any one from:*
    • Find a copyright-free graphic
    • Ask for permission
    • Pay to use it

19. (a) Pseudocode

  (b) BarBryantGla

   1 mark each for:
    • Identifying only surname entered
    • Three strings in correct order
    • No spaces as concatenated

  (c) *1 mark each for:*
    • Assignment
    • Concatenation

  (d) *Interpreter — any one from:*
    • Don't have to leave editing environment
    • Position of errors in code identified during test run

   Compiler — any one from:
    • Compiled code runs faster
    • Code is only translated once
    • Compiled code cannot be edited
    • Compiled code requires less memory to execute

  (e)

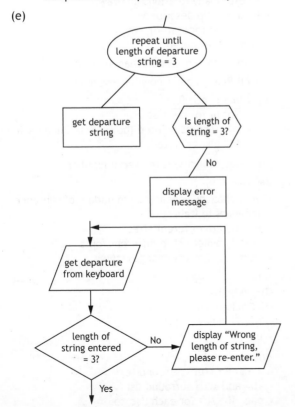

```
Start loop
Ask user to input string
If the string is not 3
characters long display error
End loop when string entered
is 3 characters in length
```

1 mark each for:
• Input of string
• Conditional loop
• Condition length = 3 characters
• Error message

20. (a) (i) To link two tables

  (ii) *1 mark for each correct row:*

	Table	Field
Primary key	Branch	branchNumber
Primary key	Car	registration
Foreign key	Car	branchNumber

  (iii) One branch has many cars

(b) *1 mark each for:*
    • Headings
    • Two correct cars identified
    • Order of two cars correct

Make	Model	Registration
Nissan	Qashqai	SH88 NNG
Volkswagen	Golf	ST99 FDT

(c) *1 mark for each correct row:*

Field(s)	model, colour, town, mileage
Table(s)	car, branch
Search criteria	model = "Ka"
Sort order	mileage ascending

21. (a) *1 mark each for:*
    • Bonus, real
    • Sales, integer

(b) *1 mark each for:*
    • Extreme — 0
    • Exception — any suitable example (<0, text)

(c) (i) Logic

  (ii) *1 mark each for:*
    • Change first condition
   To sales>10 and <= 20

  Example structure chart response for 21(c) (ii):

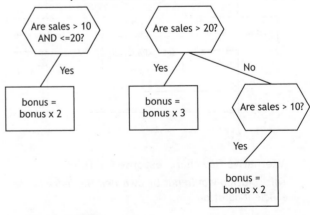

(d) (i) Register

  (ii) Arithmetic Logic Unit (ALU)